THE SENATE'S CIVIL WAR

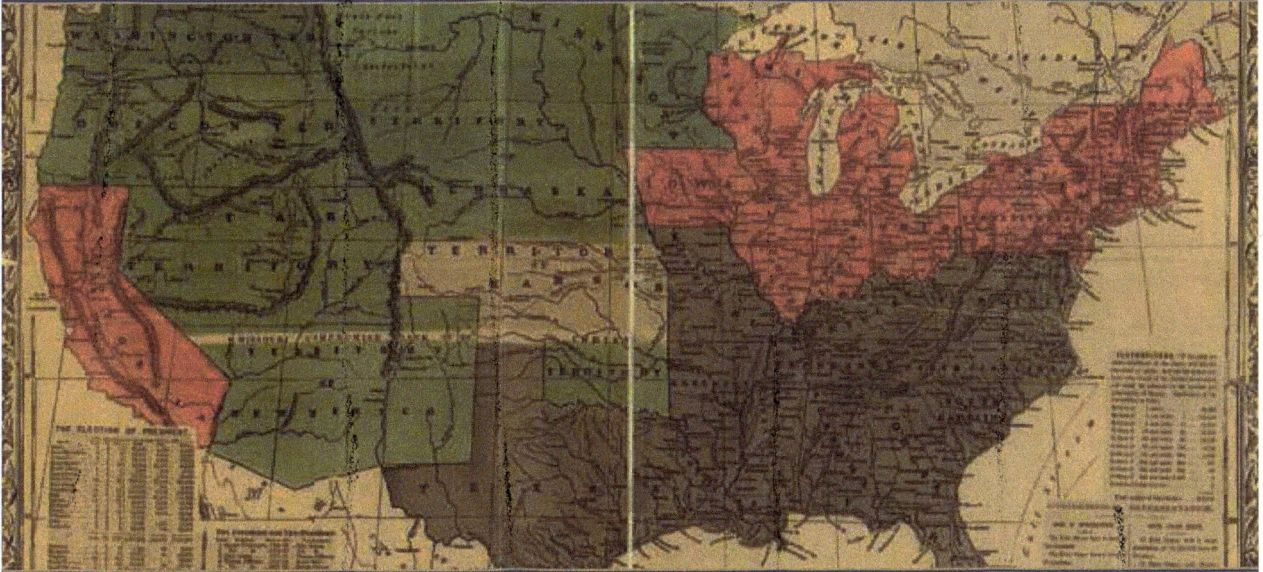

Prepared by the Senate Historical Office
Under the direction of
Nancy Erickson, Secretary of the Senate

UNITED
STATES
SENATE

THE SENATE'S CIVIL WAR

T he United States Senate played a crucial role during the Civil War. Although the history of the war is often told from the perspective of President Abraham Lincoln and his military commanders, the Senate faced war-related issues even before Lincoln took the oath of office, and continued to influence national events throughout the war. In the post-war Reconstruction years, senators led the debates over emancipation, civil rights, and the readmission of Southern states to representation, and they proposed constitutional amendments to guarantee rights of citizenship. Throughout this long period of national crisis, the Senate also fulfilled its oversight and legislative responsibilities, passing a remarkable collection of landmark bills. In commemoration of the sesquicentennial of these pivotal events, this is the story of the Senate's Civil War.

U.S. Capitol, ca. 1846.

Senator Daniel Webster of Massachusetts addressing the Senate, 1850.

CONFLICT AND COMPROMISE

Sectional disputes dominated debate during the Senate's Golden Age, the period between the Missouri Compromise of 1820 and the Compromise of 1850 that brought to the chamber a group of talented legislators and powerful orators. In the Senate, where the Constitution established an equality of states, there existed a delicate balance between North and South, slave and free states. For many years, senators crafted legislation designed to resolve sectional conflicts and avoid secession and civil war. In the 1850s, however, further efforts at compromise failed. The Senate endured a violent and turbulent decade that brought an end to its Golden Age and propelled the nation to the brink of war.

The rapid expansion of the nation, as settlers moved west and new territories applied for statehood, repeatedly raised the issue of slavery. The Constitution allowed slavery to exist in the states but left Congress to decide its status in the territories. The Northern states, having abolished slavery, sought to prevent its spread, while the Southern states, having grown more dependent on slave labor, asserted the rights of Southerners to transport their way of life into the new territories. In 1820 the Missouri Compromise drew a line across the nation at the 36th parallel, above which slavery would be prohibited, and below which it could expand. When the war with Mexico, from 1846 to 1848, resulted in vast new territories in the southwest, the debate over expansion of slavery was renewed.

In 1850 Senator Henry Clay of Kentucky introduced a package of compromise measures to relieve the sectional tensions created by territorial expansion. Aware of the controversial nature of his proposals, Clay urged his colleagues to "beware, to pause, to reflect before they lend themselves to any purposes which shall destroy that Union." On March 7, 1850, Senator Daniel Webster of Massachusetts rose from his Senate seat and declared: "I wish to speak today, not as a Massachusetts man, nor as a Northern man, but as an American . . . I speak today for the preservation of the Union." Other senators, most notably John Calhoun of South Carolina, opposed Clay's plan. With Webster's support, and with the assistance of Senator Stephen Douglas of Illinois, Congress passed revised versions of Clay's bills, which became law in September 1850. The Compromise of 1850 admitted California as a free state, left open the possibility of slavery in the territories of New Mexico and Utah, abolished the slave trade in the District of Columbia, and created a stronger fugitive slave law.

Anxious to build a transcontinental railroad from Chicago to the West Coast, Senator Douglas introduced the Kansas-Nebraska Act of 1854 to organize those territories for statehood. To meet the objections of Southerners who were promoting a southern route for the railroad, the act opened the territories for settlement, but provided that the settlers, through "popular sovereignty," could allow or prohibit slavery. This undermined the 1820 Missouri Compromise and further inflamed the passions in the North and the South. Both slaveholders and abolitionists flooded into the new territories to influence votes on state constitutions. Communities erupted into violence in what became known as "Bleeding Kansas." Intended to settle sectional disputes, the Kansas-Nebraska Act instead brought the nation closer to civil war.

In May 1856 Senator Charles Sumner, a fiery abolitionist from Massachusetts, delivered a five-hour oration in the Senate Chamber entitled "The Crime Against Kansas." Sumner's inflammatory speech was a harsh indictment of those who supported the spread of slavery

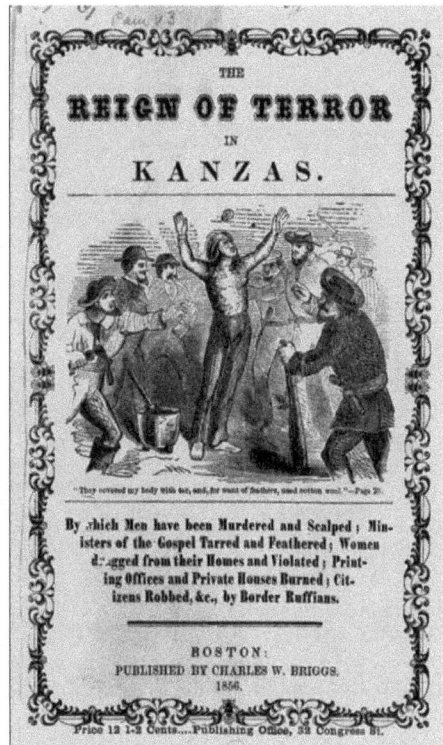

An 1856 booklet cover illustrating the violent conflicts in Kansas Territory.

SOUTHERN CHIVALRY— ARGUMENT versus CLUB'S.

A cartoon depicting Sumner's 1856 beating by Representative Preston Brooks.

and attacked several senators by name, including Andrew Butler of South Carolina. On May 22, 1856, Preston Brooks—a member of the House of Representatives and Senator Butler's relative—retaliated. After the Senate had adjourned for the day, Brooks approached Sumner at his desk in the Senate Chamber and repeatedly struck him on the head with his heavy walking stick, breaking the wooden cane into pieces. Badly injured by the attack, Sumner was able to appear in the Senate only intermittently over the next three years, as he slowly recovered. His empty desk became visible evidence that legislative compromise could no longer settle the emotional and divisive issue of slavery in the territories.

An era in Senate history ended when the Senate held its last session in its venerable old chamber. The rush of states entering the Union had doubled the number of senators and forced them to authorize construction of a new, larger chamber.

An 1860 cartoon depicting the four presidential candidates. Lincoln (far left) and Douglas are tearing apart the western part of the United States while Breckinridge (center) attacks the south; Bell (far right) tries to repair the northeastern section.

On January 4, 1859, senators marched in procession from the old chamber—so associated with the Great Triumvirate of Henry Clay, Daniel Webster, and John Calhoun—to the new chamber in the Capitol's north wing. In that procession walked men who would soon be leaders of the Union and the Confederacy.

SECESSION

The presidential election of 1860 saw a split in the Democratic Party between its northern and southern wings, and the rise of the new Republican Party. The northern Democratic senator Stephen Douglas of Illinois ran against a southern Democrat, Vice President John C. Breckinridge of Kentucky, and against the Republican candidate, Abraham Lincoln, whom Douglas had defeated for a Senate seat just two years earlier. A fourth candidate, former Whig senator John Bell of Tennessee, ran as the Constitutional Union candidate. In this divided field, Lincoln won the election on November 6, 1860. Four days later, Senator James Chesnut of South Carolina resigned his Senate seat. Although no state had yet seceded from the Union, rumors of secession were heard everywhere. Chesnut "burned his bridges" in the Senate, noted his wife Mary, and returned to South Carolina to draft an ordinance of secession and attend the first Confederate Congress. The next day, his fellow South Carolinian, Senator James Hammond, submitted his own resignation and turned his attention to establishing the Confederacy, which he pledged to support "with all the strength I have."

Senator Jefferson Davis of Mississippi.

On December 20 South Carolina voted to secede from the Union, followed by another 10 states over the next 6 months.

The month of January 1861 proved to be particularly painful for the Senate. On January 9 Mississippi became the second state to secede. This action prompted Senator Jefferson Davis to address the Senate on January 10, imploring his colleagues to allow for peaceful secession of the Southern states. "If you desire at this last moment to avert civil war, so be it," Davis proclaimed. "If you will not have it thus . . . then, gentlemen of the North, a war is to be inaugurated the like of which men have not seen. . . ." On January 21, as a packed and tearful gallery of spectators watched, Davis bid farewell to the Senate. In his final address, he warned that interference with Southern secession would be disastrous.

Abraham Lincoln's first inauguration, March 4, 1861.

I am sure I feel no hostility to you, Senators from the North. I am sure there is not one of you, whatever sharp discussion there may have been between us, to whom I cannot now say, in the presence of my God, I wish you well . . . . I hope . . . for peaceful relations with you, though we must part. . . . The reverse may bring disaster on every portion of the country . . . . Mr. President, and Senators, having made the announcement which the occasion seemed to me to require, it only remains for me to bid you a final adieu.

On February 18 Davis became president of the Confederate States of America. By that time, 7 of the 11 Confederate states had already seceded. (Tennessee became the last to withdraw, on June 8, 1861.) When crowds gathered at the Capitol on March 4, 1861, to witness Lincoln's first inauguration, the nation was already divided and preparing for war.

THE WAR BEGINS

During the months between Lincoln's election and his inauguration, many members of Congress clung to the hope of reconciliation. Kentucky senator John J. Crittenden led a last-ditch effort at compromise, proposing to extend to the Pacific Ocean the line established by the 1820 Missouri Compromise. The proposal failed. Senator Charles Sumner dismissed such compromise efforts as a misreading of the secession movement, "deeming it merely *political* & governed by the laws of such movements, to be met by reason, by concession, & by compromise; whereas it is a *revolution*."

Soon after Lincoln took office, the commander of Fort Sumter in South Carolina's Charleston Harbor reported that supplies were running low. Several members of the president's cabinet recommended evacuating the fort. Instead, the president chose to resupply it, but with food rather than with weapons. At 4:40 a.m. on April 12, 1861, Confederate cannons opened fire on Fort Sumter and Union forces surrendered 34 hours later. The attack prompted President Lincoln to issue a proclamation on April 15 calling upon Congress to convene an emergency session on July 4. He also called for 75,000 troops to protect the seat of government and suppress the rebellion—although they were asked to serve for only 90 days.

The response across the North to the president's call was swift. As one journalist recorded, Lincoln's proclamation "was received with the beating of drums and the ringing notes of the bugle, calling the defenders of the capitol to their colors. Every city and hamlet had its flag-raising." Senator John Sherman of Ohio later described this impressive reaction in his memoirs: "The response of the loyal states to the call of Lincoln was perhaps the most remarkable uprising of a great people in the history of mankind. Within a few days the road to Washington was opened, but the men who answered the call were not soldiers, but citizens, badly armed, and without drill or discipline." The first Union troops, volunteers from Pennsylvania, arrived in Washington on April 18 and were quartered in the House wing of the Capitol. The next to arrive was the Sixth Regiment from Massachusetts. Having encountered angry mobs of Southern sympathizers in Baltimore, the Massachusetts soldiers

The Sixth Regiment of Massachusetts volunteers clashing with Southern sympathizers in Baltimore.

arrived in Washington on April 19 bloodied and exhausted. They established their camp in the Senate Chamber. Longtime Senate doorkeeper Isaac Bassett described the arrival of these embattled troops:

The Sixth Regiment of Massachusetts, nine hundred strong, under the command of Col. Jones, were attacked in Baltimore on their way to Washington. . . . On arriving here these were marched into the Capitol and immediately occupied the Senate Chamber. . . . The col. made the Vice President's Room his headquarters. They looked tired I saw blood running down their faces. Their clothes were full of dust. Everything was done that could be for their comfort.

Soon Washington was teeming with soldiers, thousands making their camp in and around the Capitol. In a letter to his son on April 19, Architect of the Capitol Thomas U. Walter commented that "the Capitol itself is turned into a barracks; there

Union troops on the Capitol grounds.

will be 30,000 troops here by tomorrow night." Company E of the National Guard, a group formed from mechanics who had been working in and around the Capitol, made their quarters in the Revolutionary Claims Committee room. A young writer named Theodore Winthrop of the Seventh New York Regiment documented his experience in the *Atlantic Monthly*, published in July 1861. "Our life in the Capitol was most dramatic and sensational . . . " he wrote. "We joked, we shouted, we sang, we mounted the Speaker's desk and made speeches." Seated at the senators' desks in the still-new chamber, soldiers used Senate stationery and franked envelopes to correspond with their loved ones back home. In the Capitol Rotunda, a reporter witnessed a young member of the New York Zouaves, "a mere boy," swing nearly 100 feet on a rope from an interior cornice of the new dome. "It did not seem to be a novel feat to the others, as they noticed it no more than any ordinary occurrence," the reporter remarked. One of the soldiers' mock sessions of the Senate was witnessed by a Washington correspondent for the *Providence Journal*, who wrote:

The presiding officer was just putting the question on a resolution directing the sergeant-at-arms to proceed immediately to the White House and to request the President, if, in his opinion not incompatible with the public interest, to send down a gallon of his best brandy. A motion to strike out the word "Brandy" and substitute "Old Rye" was voted

Union troops quartered in the Rotunda of the U.S. Capitol, 1861.

down, on constitutional grounds, and because the "Hon. Senator from South Carolina" who offered it had both his legs on the desk, while the rules only permitted one. And finally a motion was made to clear the galleries as disorderly persons were looking on, evidently to ridicule the proceedings and otherwise behaving in a manner not consistent with the dignity of the Senate.

Despite the levity of these reports, emotions ran high throughout the city. In the Senate Chamber, incensed troops took their bayonets to the desk of former senator Jefferson Davis, seeking to destroy an object once occupied by the new leader of the Confederacy. Hearing the commotion,

Bassett rushed to stop the destruction of the desk, reminding the soldiers that it belonged to the United States government, not Davis. "You were put here to protect, and not to destroy!" he shouted. "They stopped immediately and said I was right, they thought it belonged to Jefferson Davis," Bassett noted in his memoirs.

A militant spirit prevailed when Congress met on July 4, 1861. The more radical members pressed the administration for quick military action. Rumors spread that President Lincoln had no intention of suppressing the rebellion and was simply delaying in order to achieve a compromise with the South. The radicals demanded a quick campaign aimed at the rebel capital of Richmond. Despite the fact that Northern troops remained untrained and untested for

This painting by celebrated American artist Stanley Meltzoff (1917-2006) depicts retreating Union troops and civilians who had come to watch the Battle of Bull Run.

battle, popular support grew for war. "On to Richmond!" read the headline in the influential *New York Tribune*: "Forward to Richmond! The Rebel Congress must not be allowed to meet there." The drumbeat of publicity persuaded Lincoln to launch an early offensive.

On Sunday, July 21, 1861, some members of Congress gathered in Centreville, Virginia, about 30 miles from Washington, to watch the Union forces march into battle at Bull Run. Civilians rode out in wagons and packed picnic lunches to enjoy while watching the battle (thus known as the "Picnic Battle"). As journalist Benjamin Perley Poore commented, spectators gathered "as they would have gone to see a horse-race or to witness a Fourth of July procession." The Union army performed well in the morning, but by early afternoon the Confederates brought

in reinforcements, staging an intense battle over a space known as Henry Hill. When Union generals finally called retreat around 4:00 p.m., the frightened soldiers fled for their lives, sweeping up civilians in their retreat back to Washington.

Near the battlefield, a group of senators were eating lunch. They heard a loud noise and looked around to see the road filled with retreating soldiers, horses, and wagons. "Turn back, turn back, we're whipped," Union soldiers cried as they ran past the spectators. Startled, Michigan senator Zachariah Chandler tried to block the road to stop the retreat. Senator Benjamin Wade of Ohio, sensing a humiliating defeat, picked up a discarded rifle and threatened to shoot any soldier who ran. While Senator Henry Wilson of Massachusetts distributed sandwiches, a Confederate shell destroyed his buggy, forcing him to escape on a stray mule. Iowa senator James Grimes barely avoided capture and vowed never to go near another battlefield. Dismayed, senators returned to Washington to deliver eyewitness accounts to a stunned President Lincoln. Only one member of Congress, New York representative Alfred Ely, made it to Richmond that day—as a prisoner of war.

The Union army's defeat at Bull Run shocked members of Congress, making it clear that the war would last much longer than 90 days and be harder fought than anyone had expected. The First Battle of Bull Run was only the beginning. It "was the worst event & the best event in our history," wrote Charles Sumner to Lincoln. It was "the worst, as it was the greatest present calamity & shame,—the best, as it made the extinction of Slavery inevitable." Congress responded to the defeat on July 29,

Senator Edward D. Baker of Oregon.

1861, by passing legislation that significantly increased the size of the army, and on August 5 by passing an act to better organize the military. These acts provided Lincoln with the largest military power ever conferred upon a president up to that time.

A week after Bull Run, Kentucky senator John C. Breckinridge rose in the Senate Chamber to oppose efforts to declare that a state of insurrection existed. "Here we have been hurling gallant fellows on to death, and the blood of Americans has been shed—for what?" he asked. "Nothing but ruin, utter ruin, to the North, to the South, to the East, to the West, will follow the prosecution of this conflict." As soon as Breckinridge took his seat, Oregon senator Edward Dickinson Baker, dressed in military uniform, rose to rebut him. An old friend of Lincoln's from Springfield, Illinois, Baker had resigned from the House of Representatives to lead troops in battle during the Mexican-American War, and had later moved to Oregon, where he was elected senator. In the spring of 1861 he had raised a "California regiment" (actually recruiting on the East Coast), and had spent that morning training his troops. "How could we make peace? Upon what terms?" Baker thundered in reply to Breckinridge. "It is our duty to advance, if we can; to suppress insurrection; to put down rebellion; to scatter the enemy; and when we have done so, to preserve in the terms of the bill, the liberty, lives, and property of the people of the country, by just and fair police regulations." Encouraged by applause from the gallery, Baker acknowledged that the war would exact a heavy price. "There will be some graves reeking with blood, watered by tears of affection." Little did Baker know that he was describing his own imminent fate.

When the Senate adjourned the extra session on August 6, 1861, some senators returned to their home states to raise regiments of soldiers. A few, like Baker, donned uniforms themselves. Although Baker turned down a commission as brigadier general so that he could remain a senator, he felt that he could engage in combat while Congress was adjourned. On October 21, 1861, Baker led a brigade of Union volunteers across the Potomac River, seeking to advance on Leesburg, Virginia. Confederate forces stopped them at Ball's Bluff, trapping them on the cliffs overlooking the river. Nearly 1,000 soldiers were killed, wounded, or captured, including Baker, the only sitting U.S. senator ever to die in combat. When the Senate next convened on December 2, 1861, Oregon senator James M. Nesmith delivered a heartfelt eulogy recalling Baker's impassioned debate with Breckinridge: "What he said as a Senator he was willing to do as a soldier."

The death of Senator Baker at the Battle of Ball's Bluff, 1861.

Within the Senate Chamber, the secession of the Southern states left a visible impact. When the Senate had convened at the start of the 37th Congress on March 4, 1861, the names of withdrawn senators whose terms had expired were ordered deleted from the Senate rolls. With the exception of Tennessee senator Andrew Johnson, who remained in the Senate after his state seceded, those Southerners whose terms continued simply stayed away. Some sent notices of withdrawal or announced their secession in local newspapers, but others just failed to appear. In July 1861 the Senate expelled 10 of the absent senators. In December it expelled Senator John C. Breckinridge, who had joined the Confederate army even though his home state of Kentucky remained in the Union. In January 1862 the Senate also expelled the two senators from Missouri, who sided with the Confederacy despite their state remaining in the Union. The final expulsion took place on February 5, 1862, when the Senate threw out Indiana senator Jesse Bright for promoting a constituent's efforts to sell arms to the Confederacy.

THE CAPITOL IN WARTIME

In just a few short weeks after the war began, Washington was transformed from a quiet capital to a city alive with the sounds of thousands of uniformed troops marching and drilling in the streets. The Capitol, with its recently added House and Senate wings and soon-to-be-completed cast-iron dome, took on "the appearance of an armed

Zouave regiment marching down Pennsylvania Avenue, Washington, D.C., ca. 1861.

fort," according to Washington writer Julia Taft Bayne. Building materials intended for the construction of the new dome were converted for use in fortifying the building. "About the entrance and between the pillars were barricades of iron plates intended for the dome, held in place by barrels of sand and cement," Bayne wrote. Inside the building, the statuary and paintings were boarded up or draped in protective coverings.

As more troops arrived, conditions in the Capitol deteriorated. "Things are more unpleasant here every day," Capitol architect Thomas Walter lamented, "every street, lane, and alley is filled with soldiers . . . the Senate Chamber is alive with lice; it makes my head itch to think of it—the bed bugs have travelled up stairs." Isaac Bassett also worried about the damage being done to the ornate structure. "It almost broke my heart to see the soldiers bring armfuls of bacon and hams and throw them down upon the floor of the marble room," he wrote. "Almost with tears in my eyes I begged them not to grease up the walls and the furniture." On May 3, 1861, Walter complained in a letter to his wife about the atrocious conditions caused by the inadequate washing facilities in the Capitol: "There are 4000 [troops] in the Capitol with all their provision, ammunition and baggage, and the smell is awful. The building is like one grand water closet— every hole and corner is defiled . . . . The stench is so terrible I have refused to take my office into the building. It is sad to see the defacement of the building every where."

Following the Second Battle of Bull Run in 1862, the Union army used the Capitol as a hospital for wounded troops, stirring sympathy among Capitol Hill personnel, but taking a toll on the building. In a letter dated September 2, 1862, Walter wrote:

> The excitement here is very great and the presence of so many wounded greatly affect the sensibilities of all who have any feeling—poor fellows, what they must suffer. . . . They have taken the Capitol as a hospital, and the beds are now up in the rotunda, the old Hall of Rep's, and the passages—one thousand beds have been put up. It does not interfere with our work in the least, and I think the move is a good one.

Walter's assessment changed considerably over the next month. On October 3, as deteriorating conditions in the Capitol forced him to take his work outdoors, he wrote: "I am now writing in

Wounded soldiers receiving treatment in the Capitol Rotunda, 1862.

the middle of the street, with clouds of dust flying around me." He lamented to a friend that he had been "compelled to move by the filth and stench, and live stock in the Capitol—there are more than 1000 sick and wounded in the building and it has become intolerable especially in the upper rooms."

To meet the needs of the soldiers, the military quartermaster constructed large brick ovens in the basement of the Capitol. Several brick-walled rooms in the basement's center section were quickly converted into a bakery to feed the troops. Interior staircases leading down to the new Capitol bakery were partially covered with planks so that huge barrels of flour could be rolled down into the basement. There were 14 ovens that baked 200 loaves a day, and another six or seven that produced 800 loaves a day. These larger ovens were located under the great steps on the west terrace of the Capitol. "The arcades under the flagway on the west side of the building are used for cooking," commented the *Washington Star*, "and the smoke may be seen pouring out of the holes in the grassy slope."

Feeding the troops became a well-organized activity. "When rations are to be served, the men pass in single file in the area along the series of arches," continued the *Star*, "each with a tin plate and a tin cup. At the first archway two slices of freshly baked bread are handed to each man; at the next arch his allowance of meat, and at the next his coffee or soup, as the case may be." While the troops and other occupants of the Capitol soon became accustomed to the aroma of baking bread, others worried about

The Capitol's bakery operations in 1862.

the conditions created by having such a large bakery housed in the Capitol. "I am pained to see a treasure instructed to my care—a treasure money cannot replace—receiving great damage from the smoke and soot that penetrates everywhere through that part of the Capitol which is under my charge," wrote the librarian of Congress, John G. Stephenson, who worried about the threat of fire to his books that were housed in the Capitol.

When the Senate convened its emergency session in July 1861, and then returned for its regular session in December, soldiers quartered in the Capitol were forced to find another home, joining the thousands of troops occupying the city. "During the entire war Washington was a military camp," Senator Sherman recalled in his memoirs.

In fact, the city was surrounded by 68 forts and 22 batteries by war's end, making it one of the most heavily fortified cities in the world. Sherman continued:

It was quite a habit of Senators and Members, during the war, to call at the camps of soldiers from their respective states. It was my habit, while Congress was in session during the war, to ride on horseback over a region within ten miles of Washington. . . . I became familiar with every lane and road, and especially with camps and hospitals. At the time it could truly be said that Washington was a great camp and hospital.

Despite the wartime emergency, work progressed on the new dome for the

The installation of the Statue of Freedom nearing completion, 1863.

Capitol. The War Department announced on May 15, 1861, that it could not ensure funding for completion of the dome, but the workers agreed to continue without pay. At Clark Mills's foundry, which was commissioned to cast Thomas Crawford's Statue of Freedom for the top of the new dome, an enslaved man named Philip Reid was among those preparing this crowning symbol for the nation's Capitol. Reid was one of many slaves who had labored in the construction of the Capitol. When the statue was finally placed atop the dome on December 2, 1863, Reid was a free man, liberated by the District of Columbia Compensated Emancipation Act in 1862. The installation of the Statue of Freedom proved to be a symbolic event, signifying the enduring nation in a time of civil war. A battery of artillery fired a salute of 35 rounds, representing every state in the Union, including those of the Confederacy. The salute was then returned by the many forts surrounding the city of Washington.

THE JOINT COMMITTEE ON THE CONDUCT OF THE WAR

The defeat at Bull Run in 1861 was the first in a series of military disasters for the Union. As casualities mounted, including the loss of Senator Baker at Ball's Bluff, many Americans in and out of Congress demanded explanations. In the opening days of the 37th Congress in 1861, the public and elected officials called for an inquiry into events surrounding the dramatic defeats suffered by the Union army. Senator William Pitt Fessenden of Maine articulated the thoughts of many when he said, "We see many things done which do not meet the public approbation. We see some things done which we do not approve ourselves, and which evidently call for an investigation, or, at any rate, call for such an explanation as shall satisfy the people."

In that spirit, Senator Zachariah Chandler introduced a resolution on December 5, 1861, to investigate the battles at Bull Run and Ball's Bluff, while other senators demanded a broad inquiry into the conduct of the war. Consequently, Senator James Grimes amended the resolution, calling for a joint committee to examine all aspects of the war. The concurrent resolution, passed on December 10, 1861, created a joint committee composed of three senators and four representatives and granted its members the power to "inquire into the conduct of the present war and to send for persons and papers." Five Republicans and two Democrats served on the committee, reflecting Republican control of the Civil War Congress.

Traditionally, the senator who proposed the resolution chaired the committee, but Chandler deferred to his close friend and colleague Senator Benjamin Wade, believing that the Ohioan's legal background made him particularly well suited for directing the investigation.

At its first meeting, members of the joint committee agreed to keep their deliberations secret. Meeting in a Senate committee room, the joint committee held no public hearings and forbade those who testified from speaking with the press. Committee members, however, regularly broke their own rules by leaking information to the newspapers to generate public support for their efforts. In March 1862, for example, committee members leaked the written statement of General John C. Frémont, commander of the Western Department and a favorite of the committee, to the *New York Daily Tribune*.

They hoped to enlist public opinion behind General Frémont's controversial actions in the field, and to draw upon this well of public support to lobby Lincoln for Frémont's reappointment.

Abolitionists known as "Radical Republicans" dominated the committee and frequently criticized the president's war strategy for not being aggressive enough on the issue of slavery. Senator Wade, irritated by the president's gradual approach to emancipation and equality for African Americans, dismissed Lincoln as "a fool." The joint committee itself faced criticism from Washington insiders who denounced its work as misguided and ill-informed. Critics noted that the joint committee was well-intentioned, but that its members had no military experience and seemed unqualified to analyze war-related decisions and the commanders who made them. Some military leaders dismissed

Senator Zachariah Chandler of Michigan.

Senator Benjamin Wade of Ohio.

Major General George McClellan (center) and other military commanders, targets of the Joint Committee on the Conduct of the War.

the inquiry as partisan or ideological and not in the nation's best interest. Washington journalist Benjamin Perley Poore denounced the committee as "a mischievous organization, which assumed dictatorial powers."

Regardless of such criticism, the Joint Committee on the Conduct of the War pursued a broad investigatory agenda. In addition to examining failed military campaigns, the committee scrutinized a number of wide-ranging issues, including corruption in military supply contracts, the mistreatment of Union prisoners by Confederate forces, the massacre of Cheyenne Indians, Union trade activities, and gunboat construction, to name just a few. The joint committee worked through two Congresses, meeting 272 times over four years. Subcommittees were formed to maximize time and resources and meet with as many witnesses as possible. Members frequently traveled outside of Washington, D.C., recording testimony from witnesses and making firsthand assessments of the war effort.

Despite Senator Wade's withering assessment of Lincoln, the joint committee maintained friendly relations with the executive branch. Both President Lincoln and his successor Andrew Johnson (a former member of the joint committee), and their cabinets, complied with committee requests for meetings and access to information. Members of the joint committee frequently blamed military commanders for Union losses, often accusing them of disloyalty to the government, and they pressed for changes in military command. They strongly encouraged Lincoln to remove Major General George McClellan from command of the Army of the Potomac after successive losses early in the war. The president eventually relieved McClellan in November 1862, but he did so on his own terms, and largely disregarded the joint committee's recommendations. The joint committee proved more convincing in another case, however, and the president acquiesced to its demands that he approve the arrest and imprisonment of Brigadier General Charles Pomeroy Stone. The

General Charles Pomeroy Stone with his daughter.

committee had long questioned Stone's loyalty and blamed him for Union defeats.

The Joint Committee on the Conduct of the War produced volumes of copious reports based on its field work and the testimony of dozens of witnesses. Published periodically throughout the committee's four-year tenure, these reports were often summarized in newspapers. Nevertheless, compared to other congressional investigations, the work of the Joint Committee on the Conduct of the War remained mostly unknown to the American public. Despite this low-profile status, the committee's investigations fulfilled the congressional responsibility for oversight during a time of national crisis. Committee members felt satisfied that

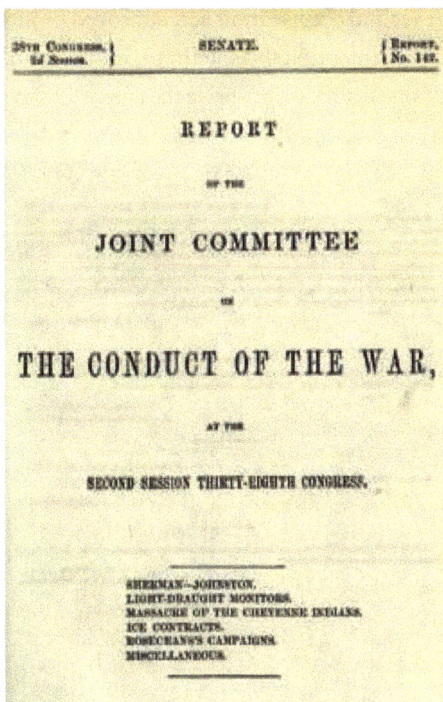

An 1865 report of the Joint Committee on the Conduct of the War.

their inquiry prompted President Lincoln to more carefully consider the strategy and evaluate the performance of his top field commanders. Interviews with military commanders provided detailed accounts of action in the field, while creating a record of wartime events that otherwise would not have been recorded.

LEGISLATIVE WORK CONTINUES

As the Senate faced the military challenges of the Civil War, senators also fulfilled their legislative responsibilities by dealing with the economic consequences of the war effort. Senator John Sherman observed that the country's greatest challenge "was not whether we could muster men, but whether we could raise money. We had to create a system of finance that would secure an enlarged revenue." Finance Committee chairman William Pitt Fessenden, who confessed his "great anxiety" about creating revenue streams to prevent the nation from becoming "bankrupt, [with] specie payments suspended, and the government living on its own discredited notes," worked feverishly to draft legislation to avert a crisis. Under Senator Fessenden's leadership, the Finance Committee sponsored bills that proved vital to funding the war. The Revenue Act of 1861 established the first federal income tax. A second revenue act, which became law on July 1, 1862, created the Bureau of Internal Revenue within the Treasury Department and established taxes on some luxury items. Senator James Blaine of Maine later called it "one of the most searching, thorough, comprehensive

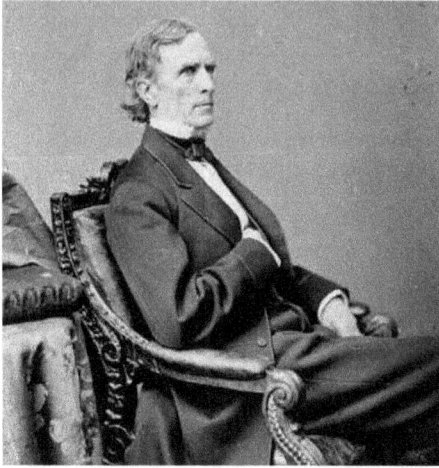

Senator William Pitt Fessenden of Maine.

systems of taxation ever devised by any Government." A third piece of revenue legislation became law on June 30, 1864, increasing the progressive income tax rates established in 1862 and adding a tax to some consumer goods including tobacco products.

Another persistent challenge was the low number of men volunteering to serve in the Union army. Senator Henry Wilson, chairman of the Committee on Military Affairs, sponsored the Conscription Act of 1863, which established the first national draft system and required registration by every male citizen and immigrant who had applied for citizenship between the ages of 20 and 45. The *New York Times* called the Conscription Act "the condition of victory," but many people criticized the law because it provided an exemption for those who could pay a $300 fee. Some critics argued that the law punished the poor, while others insisted that it interfered with states' rights, since state-based militias had fought in previous wars. However,

even with such conscription laws, both the Union and Confederate armies continued to rely mostly upon volunteers.

Eager to equip the Union army with the tools it needed to succeed, senators pushed for legislation to punish the rebels and assist Union troops. "I would do everything to strike at the rebel; confiscate their land, their houses, their slaves, anything," declared Senator Sherman. "When they take up arms against this Government, when they commit the act of rebellion, they forfeit their lives by the Constitution of the United States; they lose everything." To punish rebelling states, Senator Lyman Trumbull of Illinois sponsored confiscation acts, the first of which was signed into law on August 6, 1861, and allowed Union forces to seize all property used to aid the Confederate cause. A second confiscation act, approved in July 1862, intentionally sought to, in the words of one historian, "deprive the enemy of slave

New York draft rioters protesting the 1863 Conscription Act.

Joining of the Central Pacific and Union Pacific railroad lines to create the first transcontinental railroad, 1869.

labor." It granted the Union army the ability to seize the property, including slaves, of anyone who supported the rebel cause. The *New York Times* declared the measure a "military necessity," since enslaved persons could be seized and "use[d] to our advantage in behalf of the Union."

The Senate was also remarkably productive in enacting legislation not connected to military needs, including passage of landmark legislation for the homestead settlement of western lands, the expansion of railroad lines, and the establishment of land-grant colleges. Throughout the war years, the Senate operated, according to Senator Sherman, like "a laborious committee where bills are drawn as well as discussed." For decades Congress had argued over such issues, only to have them blocked by states' rights

advocates, largely from the South. Northern senators therefore took advantage of the absence of the Southern lawmakers to pass a series of historic bills that previously had fallen victim to sectional conflict.

Since the rapid settlement of the western territories in the 1850s, most members of Congress agreed on the need for efficient rail transport to the Pacific coast, but which route would the railroad follow? Competition between Northern and Southern members, who sought a route advantageous to their own region's interests, had prevented the Senate from passing any proposed legislation. After the South seceded, Congress agreed on a northern route to the Pacific and used federal lands to subsidize the construction of a railroad and telegraph line with the Pacific Railway Act. The bill, which became law on July 1, 1862, provided government incentives to assist "men of talent, men of character, men who are willing to invest" in developing the nation's first transcontinental rail line. President Lincoln signed a second railroad bill, the Northern Pacific Railway Act, on July 2, 1864, providing government support for the development of a second route to the Pacific from Minnesota to Oregon. Such legislation led to the successful completion of the transcontinental railroad, and on May 10, 1869, workers drove in the "Golden Spike" at Promontory, Utah—a powerful symbol of the nation's reunification.

To help develop the American West and spur economic growth, Congress passed the Homestead Act of 1862, which provided 160 acres of federal land to anyone who agreed to farm the land. The act distributed millions of acres of western land

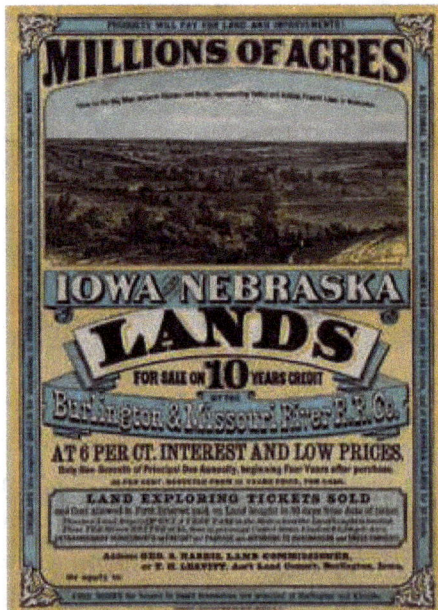

Poster advertising inexpensive land to homesteaders, 1862.

to individual settlers. Similar legislation, the Southern Homestead Act of 1866, offered the same promise to loyal Southerners and freedmen who could settle public lands. Passage of these acts encouraged farming of more land during the war years, and continued to do so for decades to come. By 1890 the federal government had granted 373,000 homesteads on some 48 million acres of undeveloped land.

Senator Justin S. Morrill of Vermont left his name on one of the most significant pieces of wartime legislation. First proposed when Morrill was serving in the House of Representatives, the Morrill Land Grant College Act of 1862 set aside federal lands to create colleges to "benefit the agricultural and mechanical arts." The president signed the bill into law on July 2, 1862. It granted each state 30,000 acres of western land, to be distributed by each senator and representative, and funded the construction of agricultural and mechanical schools. Early land-grant schools included the University of Wisconsin, Iowa State University, the State University of New Jersey (Rutgers), and the University of Missouri.

Emancipation remained foremost in the minds of legislators throughout the war years. Many senators believed that only the president had the power to emancipate slaves in the states, but as Senator Sherman explained, "Little doubt was felt as to the power of Congress to abolish slavery in the District." Consequently, on April 3, 1862, the Senate passed the District of Columbia Compensated Emancipation Act, originally sponsored by Senator Henry Wilson.

Washingtonians celebrating DC Emancipation Day, 1866.

Harper's Weekly reported that the "bill passed by a vote of twenty-nine yeas to fourteen nays. The announcement of the result was received with applause from the galleries." President Lincoln signed the bill into law on April 16, freeing slaves in the District and compensating owners up to $300 for each freeperson. The *Hartford Daily Courant* celebrated that "Not a slave exists in the District of Columbia. . . . Their shackles have fallen, never to be restored." In the months following the enactment of the law, commissioners approved more than 930 petitions, granting freedom to 2,989 slaves. "DC Emancipation Day" has been celebrated in the District of Columbia each year since 1862.

In September 1862 Lincoln announced his intention to emancipate slaves located in states "in rebellion." On January 1, 1863, the Emancipation Proclamation granted freedom to slaves residing in Confederate states not occupied by Union forces. Once emancipated the question remained, what were those formerly enslaved persons going to do? The "slaves of this country are or are soon to be free," commented Senator Lot Morrill of Maine. "Another great fact is that they are unprovided for . . . . Are they to exist in this unorganized, unprovided condition?" Following a long and difficult debate, the House and Senate passed a bill to create a Bureau for the Relief of Freedmen and Refugees—"The Freedmen's Bureau." The new agency provided food, shelter, clothing, and land to displaced Southerners, including newly freed African Americans.

23

Although President Lincoln's Emancipation Proclamation ended the practice of slavery in rebellious states in 1863, at war's end in 1865 the question of slavery had not been resolved. The federal government required new state constitutions in former Confederate states to include abolition of slavery, but there was nothing to prevent states from reinstituting the practice with revised state constitutions in the years to come. The only way to make the abolition of slavery permanent was to pass an amendment to the Constitution. A group of senators, including Lyman Trumbull of Illinois, Charles Sumner of Massachusetts, and John Henderson of Missouri, sponsored resolutions for a constitutional amendment to abolish slavery nationwide. On April 8, 1864, the Senate voted 38 to 6 to pass the amendment, and the House followed suit on January 31, 1865, with a vote of 119 to 56. The Thirteenth Amendment, ratified by the states on December 6, 1865, abolished slavery "within the United States, or any place subject to their jurisdiction."

UNION VICTORY AND NATIONAL TRAGEDY

The war's end was in sight when President Lincoln delivered his second inaugural address on March 4, 1865. Crowds gathered on the muddy Capitol grounds while ceremonies marking the start of a new Congress took place in the Senate Chamber. Following the inauguration of Vice President Andrew Johnson and the swearing in of senators, all proceeded through the Rotunda to the eastern portico of the Capitol. With the now-

SUNDAY NIGHT'S REPORT.

VERY LATEST.

HANG OUT YOUR BANNERS.

FIRE YOUR GREAT GUNS!

VICTORY!

The Great Rebellion About Squelched.

MOST IMPORTANT EVENT OF THE WAR.

The Carpet Bag Government Coming to Grief.

LEE'S WHOLE ARMY SURRENDERED !!

Unconditional Surrender Dictates the Terms.

THE TERMS.

Backbone of the Rebellion Broken.

THE LAST DITCH IN SIGHT.

The Pins of the Confederacy Knocked from Under.

DEO GRATIAS !

The *Daily Cleveland Herald* announcing Union victory, April 10, 1865.

completed dome towering above him, the president made his appeal to the country to move forward, "with malice toward none . . . to bind up the nation's wounds." One month later, the war was over.

On April 4, 1865, as news of the fall of Richmond spread, public buildings throughout Washington were illuminated in celebration. "The Capitol made a magnificent display—as did the whole city. . . . It was indeed glorious, *all Washington* was in the streets," wrote Benjamin Brown French, commissioner of public buildings in Washington, D.C. To celebrate the event, French "had the 23rd verse of the 118th Psalm printed on cloth, in enormous letters, as a transparency, and stretched on a frame the entire length of the top of the western portico, . . . 'This is the Lord's doing; it is marvelous in our eyes.'" A week later, after Confederate General Robert E. Lee surrendered at Appomattox, crowds of Washingtonians again took to the streets in jubilation. Secretary of War Edwin Stanton ordered that guns be fired in salute to commemorate the day.

The euphoria of Union victory came to a sudden halt on the night of April 14, 1865, when President Lincoln was shot while attending a play at Ford's Theater. As the president lay dying in a house across the street from the theater, Senator Charles Sumner appeared at his bedside. Keeping his deathbed vigil throughout the long night, the Massachusetts senator was one of the few present when Lincoln died on the morning of April 15. "Mourn not the dead," Sumner later wrote in his

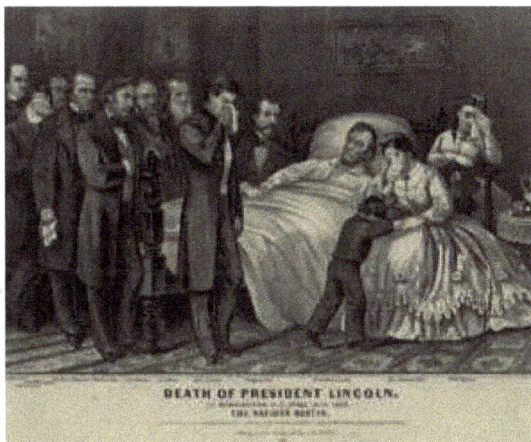

Senator Sumner and others keeping vigil at the deathbed of Abraham Lincoln, April 14, 1865.

eulogy to Lincoln, "but rejoice in his life and example . . . . Rejoice that through him Emancipation was proclaimed." Having just days before taken to the streets in joyful celebration, Washingtonians now solemnly lined Pennsylvania Avenue as the massive funeral procession made its way to the Capitol. In the Rotunda, the body of the martyred president lay in state upon a hastily constructed catafalque. Reporter Benjamin Perley Poore described the dramatic scene:

The procession was two hours and ten minutes in passing a given point, and was about three miles long. The centre of it had reached the Capitol and was returning before the rear had left Willard's [Hotel]. In one single detachment were over six thousand civil employees of the Government. Arriving at the Capitol, the remains were placed in the centre of the rotunda, beneath the mighty dome, which had been draped in mourning inside and out.

The Grand Review of the Union armies in Washington, D.C., May 23, 1865.

The death of the president muted the celebrations of Union victory. "It seems even yet a frightful dream, rather than a reality," said Senator James Dixon of Connecticut, "in the hour when his wisdom and his patriotism were about to be crowned with the success they deserved." With the prospects for peace finally at hand, Dixon thought it especially tragic that Lincoln, "the humane, the forgiving, the patient, the forbearing, has been stricken down by the hand of an assassin. That voice is silent." The Capitol was still draped in mourning in late May when Washingtonians witnessed the Grand Review of the Union armies. The Senate doorkeeper, Isaac Bassett, captured these emotional two days in his diary:

No nation ever looked on such a triumphal procession as railed through the 150,000 strong and twenty miles at least in length. The soldiers were returning from the longest marches, the severest exposures which any armies in modern times have passed through, their tattered banners told the tale of their prolonged hardships. This was no holiday parade of soldiers. Here were our fellow citizens who had for four long woeful years left home and all that makes home dear and risked all. Sacrificed for law and liberties for us and our children. . . . As far as the eye could see up Pennsylvania Avenue seemed like a river of life. . . . There were the old banners first blessed at home and consecrated with the prayers of wives and mothers. Now shorn to shreds, scarce able to cling to the flagstaff. How glad they seem to be—their work well done, their homes secure, their nation saved.

RECONSTRUCTION

Long before the Union victory, Congress had been preparing for the many challenges the nation would face at war's end, particularly the integration of four million newly emancipated African Americans into the political life of the nation. Led by the Radical Republicans in the House and Senate, Congress passed the Wade-Davis bill on July 2, 1864—co-sponsored by Senator Benjamin Wade of Ohio and Representative Henry Davis of Maryland—to provide for the admission to representation of rebel states upon meeting certain conditions. Among the conditions was the requirement that 50 percent of white males in the state swear a loyalty oath, and the insistence that the state grant African American men the right to vote. President Lincoln, who had earlier proposed a more modest 10-percent threshold, pocket-vetoed the Wade-Davis bill, stating he was opposed to being "inflexibly committed to any single plan of restoration." When the 38th Congress came to an end on March 3, 1865, the president and members of Congress had not yet reached an agreement on the terms of Reconstruction. Then, on April 9, General Lee surrendered. Less than a week later President Lincoln was assassinated and Vice President Andrew Johnson, a former senator from Tennessee, became president.

President Johnson implemented his own reconstruction plan during the summer of 1865. Eager to include Southern states, he appointed provisional governors, many of whom were former Confederates, and empowered them to call state constitutional conventions. After ratifying new constitutions and electing new state governments, Johnson promised that the states could regain full federal recognition within the Union. A former slaveholder, the president did not support black suffrage. When the 39th Congress convened on December 4, 1865, some of the newly elected legislators from former Confederate states presented credentials, expecting to be seated in the Senate. Questions about the validity of the credentials prompted the House and Senate to establish a Joint Committee on Reconstruction. This 15-member committee, composed of nine representatives and six senators, investigated "the conditions of the States which formed the so-called confederate States of America"

President Andrew Johnson.

to determine whether they "are entitled to be represented in either House of Congress." Following its investigation, the committee refused to admit the Southern members.

Both moderates and radicals in Congress opposed the president's lenient reconstruction plan. Many Republicans, such as Representative Thaddeus Stevens of Pennsylvania and Senator William Pitt Fessenden, demanded that rebel states be admitted to representation only after adopting state constitutions that provided full citizenship to African Americans and granted black men the right to vote. The president's plan, explained Senator Timothy Howe of Wisconsin, seemed "to deny to the Senate of the United States certain prerogatives," including its constitutional right to "be the judge of the Elections, Returns and Qualifications of its own members." Senator Fessenden argued that the president's position implied that "Congress, as at present organized, has no right to pass any bill affecting the interests of the late confederate States while they

Harper's Weekly portrayal of an African American voting for the first time following passage of the Reconstruction Act of 1867, with a sneering Andrew Johnson (left) holding his suffrage veto.

are not represented in Congress." To the contrary, Fessenden insisted, "I could not rest . . . if I yielded for a moment to the idea, come from what source it may, that anybody but Congress had the right . . . to settle preliminarily the question whether the States that sent them here were entitled to have Senators and Representatives or not."

The Senate responded with its own reconstruction bills. Senator Lyman Trumbull introduced the Freedman's Bureau Bill in 1865, which extended the provisions of the earlier Freedmen's Bureau by expanding the power of military governors to enforce provisions to protect African Americans. The bill also defined the organization of interim governments under conditions prescribed by Congress. President Johnson vetoed the bill. He resisted all congressionally driven reconstruction programs, denouncing those who stood "opposed to the restoration of the Union," and calling the "indefinite or permanent exclusion of any part of the country" an "unwise and dangerous course." He urged Congress to restore representation to the 11 states of the rebellion, arguing that they were "entitled to enjoy their constitutional rights as members of the Union."

The president clashed again with Congress over Senator Trumbull's Civil Rights bill, a proposal to confer citizenship on African Americans and grant them equal protection under the law. Even moderate Senate Republicans believed the bill was, in John Sherman's words, "clearly right." The bill prompted another presidential veto, but in April 1866 both

The impeachment trial of President Andrew Johnson in the Senate Chamber, 1868.

houses mustered sufficient votes to override the veto. The Civil Rights Act, which set the foundation for the Fourteenth Amendment to the Constitution, granted citizenship and due process of law to every person born in the United States. Congress's ability to override Johnson's veto emboldened its members. Senator James Grimes declared that the "President has no power to control or influence anybody and legislation will be carried on entirely regardless of his opinions or wishes."

The following year Congress passed the Reconstruction Act of 1867, establishing the terms of formal Reconstruction and admission to representation. In order to protect African Americans and their property, that bill divided the former Confederate states, except for Tennessee, into five military districts. Each state was required to

write a new constitution, which needed to be approved by a majority of voters—including African Americans—in that state. In addition, each state was required to ratify the Thirteenth and Fourteenth Amendments. After meeting these criteria, the former Confederate states could gain full recognition and federal representation. The act became law on March 2, 1867, after Congress again overrode a presidential veto. Admission to representation of the Confederate states began the next year, with Arkansas leading the way on June 22, 1868. Formal Reconstruction had begun.

The battles over Reconstruction-era policies severely strained relations between the executive and legislative branches. Throughout 1866 and 1867, Radical Republicans in the House considered impeaching the uncompromising president.

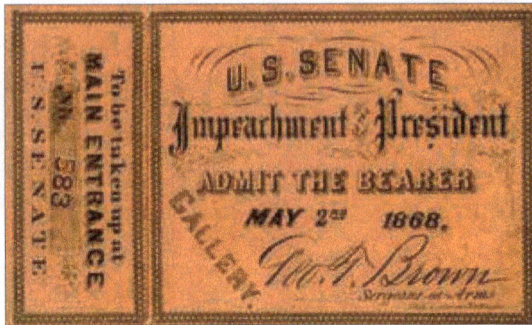

Admission ticket to the Senate galleries for the impeachment trial.

After Johnson defied the Tenure of Office Act—a congressional attempt at keeping Lincoln appointees in office—the House impeached him on February 24, 1868, sending 11 articles of impeachment to the Senate. The first presidential impeachment trial in U.S. history began when the Senate convened as a High Court of Impeachment on March 5, 1868. This unprecedented event resulted in a public spectacle, with so many people seeking to view the proceedings that for the first time, the Senate had to issue tickets for admission to its galleries.

After nearly two months of dramatic testimony, on May 16 the Senate conducted a "test" vote on the 11th article of impeachment. Seven Republicans joined all of the Democrats to support Johnson and voted not guilty, resulting in a roll-call vote of 36 guilty to 19 not guilty—one vote short of the necessary two-thirds vote required by the Constitution to convict the president and remove him from office. Subsequent votes on two other articles produced identical results. Despite the high level of frustration with President Johnson's tactics, 19 senators concluded that the president's actions did not warrant removal. "I cannot agree to destroy the harmonious working of the Constitution," explained Senator Grimes, "for the sake of getting rid of an unacceptable President." With conviction on other articles even less likely, the Republican majority adjourned the court of impeachment *sine die* and the trial of the president ended.

Congressional Reconstruction continued for another decade, producing such

The First African American members of Congress; Senator Hiram Revels of Mississippi is on the far left.

Senator Blanche K. Bruce of Mississippi.

Senator Charles S. Thomas of Colorado.

Senator Francis E. Warren of Wyoming.

notable legislative achievements as the establishment of the Department of Justice (1870), the Force Acts of 1870 and 1871, and the Civil Rights Act of 1875. The greatest successes of this period included establishment of citizenship and voting rights through the Fourteenth and Fifteenth Amendments to the Constitution. A visible sign of progress during the Reconstruction era was the election of African Americans to Congress. On February 25, 1870, onlookers in the Senate galleries cheered as Hiram Revels of Mississippi strode into the Senate Chamber to take the oath of office as the first African American senator. In 1875 Senator Blanche K. Bruce of Mississippi became the first African American to serve a full term and, on February 14, 1879, the first to preside over the Senate. Bruce had a personal background that no other senator, before or since, could claim: he had been born into slavery. Despite its accomplishments, the legacy of congressional Reconstruction was mixed, for it failed to fully establish equal rights for all citizens.

AFTERMATH

Throughout the tumultuous Civil War years the Senate remained steadfast in fulfilling its constitutional duties. It took the initiative in completing landmark legislation and providing congressional oversight of the executive branch. Senators also continued to shape important national issues in the aftermath of war, especially the evolving debate over civil rights in America.

Influencing such debates were the memories of war and Reconstruction that lingered as 63 Confederate and 81 Union veterans became U.S. senators. The last Civil War veterans were Charles S. Thomas, who had been born in Georgia and fought for the Confederacy, then served as a senator from Colorado until 1921, and Francis E. Warren, who won the Congressional Medal of Honor while fighting for the Union. He served as a senator from Wyoming until his death in 1929.

Civil War veterans also filled positions as Senate officers and staff. As late as 1911 the Senate adopted a resolution that any staff member who served in the Union army

Part of the Capitol Rotunda frieze symbolizing peace and reunification at the end of the Civil War.

and was not otherwise provided for could retain his post until he voluntarily retired. Subsequently, an "Old Soldier's Roll" appeared in the Senate patronage reports.

As the effects of the war continued to reverberate through American political life, the Capitol became a venue for displaying symbols of reconciliation. Congress purchased a statue of Abraham Lincoln in 1871. In 1899 the Grand Army of the Republic contributed a likeness of General Ulysses S. Grant. In 1909 Virginia sent to the Capitol a marble statue of General Robert E. Lee. Mississippi donated a bronze likeness of Confederate president Jefferson Davis in 1928. The statues of many Civil War era soldiers and statesmen still line the corridors of the Capitol, where they stand as a reminder of the nation's worst crisis, as a testament to the reuniting of the nation, and in recognition of the Senate's pivotal role in the wartime experience.

May 13
1861

www.ingramcontent.com/pod-product-compliance
Lightning Source LLC
Chambersburg PA
CBHW062109090426
42741CB00015B/3378